Instructions to Xu Fengqin

BY WU HSIN WITH TRANSLATION BY ROY MELVYN

The Illumination of Wu Hsin:
Volume Three – Instructions to Xu Fengqin

Translated by Roy Melvyn
Copyright 2015 Roy Melvyn

Summa Iru Publishing
Boulder, Colorado 80020

Table of Contents

Forward 5
First Day 9
Awakening 13
Self Reference 19
The Energy 40
Source and Its Objects 46
Effort 56
Experience 72
World 77
Recognition 82
Thoughts in Mind 88
Confusion 104
Final Day 107

*Wrong remedies applied cannot produce right solutions:
Cooking oil is not a cure for headache.*

Forward

This book is not a translation in the conventional sense. That is, it's not the work of a professional scholar making relatively literal renderings in English, of texts that were written or spoken in a different language. Because the texts themselves were not constructed on the basis of English grammar, they cannot, if they are to be rightly and fully understood, be presented in a mere word-for-word translation.

Rather, my work must be viewed as much as an interpretation as a translation.

Instructions to Xu Fengqin is Wu Hsin's most concise teaching, characterized by an immediacy and openness that is his hallmark.

He explains that the Absolute is where everything that comes and goes ultimately goes. It provides the potentiality for experience, whereas the Self provides the actuality.

All forms of existence equally express the underlying Ground as simultaneously within and without, both the root and the fruit of the tree.

Just as waves, bubbles and foam are distinct yet one with the ocean, there exists a primal underlying identity in difference. All that exists, according to Master Wu Hsin, is the total functioning of Grand Unity, 'datong', the Ultimate, the Absolute, the only Reality, the Ground of Being.

As a flower would have to be external to itself in order to enjoy its own fragrance, Noumenon must externalize in order to experience Itself.

However, Noumenon and phenomena remain forever a unity. The One is then both the enjoyer and the object of enjoyment, both the experiencer and the object of experience. It swallows everything in Its path.

It is the source of the reflection that we call 'world'. What we commonly refer to as 'I' does not point to the separate individual but to the non-dual Ground that underlies it.

It is devoid of all forms and it is in whose light all gods of stone and metal dissolve.

> *All sentient life flows from the same source.*
> *It can be said to be uncreated insofar as*
> *It is not a creation separate from a creator.*
> *It is an emanation,*
> *An objective expression of the Subject.*

It is wherein there is the unmoving, unknowable precondition of all activity. It is That which is without ever being noticed. It is That which so surpasses the measure of man's intellect that there can be no real knowledge of It.

Wu Hsin goes on to explain that the Energy has been granted dominion over the transitory by the Absolute and that the Mind is the working principle of the Energy.

The Energy is the agent of the Ground of Being, through which knowing, observing and acting occur. 'I am' then heralds the world. It contains the world and the instrument for the experiencing of it.

The source and substance of all action is this Energy. If there is no thread, there is no cloth. When this is seen clearly, there is no compulsion for doing or not doing anything. There is only the allowing and acceptance of whatever manifests.

His dissection of the self-reference is easy to grasp: As long as one continues to conceive of oneself as an entity, as 'I am this', one is powerless to bring about transformation because 'I am this' must always remain 'this' to insure its continuity.

What is referred to as 'I' in day-to-day parlance is simply the sense of continuity, a series of mental, sensory, physical, emotional, and perceptual impressions, created by the nervous system and embellished by a narrative attached to it.

'Me' and 'mine' provide the circumference for 'I' in the same way that banks delineate a river. However, any circumference is itself limitation. As such, to transcend limitation, 'me' and 'mine', the pervasive identification with and attachment to perceivables, must be transcended.

Contrary to the style of his time, Wu Hsin insists that there is no need for 'gongfu', or spiritual practice. Ultimately, all concepts and all dogmas, have to go, even his own.

Most of the ancient tradition of enlightenment or awakening consists of programs of practice, techniques of all kinds and philosophical expositions. However, the core of this 'daxue' or great teaching of Realization is an intuition that cannot be manufactured.

Awakening is not facilitated via conflict. Therefore, 'declaring war on' or 'killing the ego' or active suppression of mind is not the answer.

The ultimate practice is unintentional. It arises from an unseen source at an unpredictable time at a place not previously disclosed. Have faith in the Self until you recognize the Self to be your own Self. What needs to make itself known is 'ziran', or spontaneously emergent, and It does so in Its own time.

Anyone can do this.

The Master's words on these pages are like swords, cutting through thought. His instructions are a special transmission that allow one to peer directly into one's true nature, 'chien-hsing', to see the essence.

This true nature is perpetually free awareness. Wu Hsin likens it to a silent observer that watches through the body's sensory system, yet is impartial to what it sees. The word "wisdom" in Chinese is composed of two characters: 'zhi' and 'hui', knowing and the light. Knowing the light is wisdom.

Questioning is by the intellect and answers are for the intellect. The intellect cannot discern what is antecedent to it and is therefore the wrong tool for the task. That's why Wu Hsin discourages Xu Fengqin from endless questioning and advises his disciple to limit his questioning, to primarily just listen, listen without using his intellect.

You listen to the teacher and make his point of view your own. This is the Way of Wu Hsin: resonating with the teacher, being receptive and following his instructions totally.

It is not on Wu Hsin that the understanding depends
But on the listener.
Although one makes no effort to hear,
One must exert great effort to listen.

If you are not listening to Wu Hsin,
What you hear doesn't matter.
If you listen correctly, everything will happen.
Therefore keep questioning to a minimum:
Just listen.

This is his invitation, enter for a while and just listen.

First Day

Today, your instruction commences Xu Fengqin.
The instruction of Wu Hsin is
The jade of the highest value and must be treated accordingly.

Upon entering this chamber each time,
Sit and quietly establish yourself within yourself.

It is not on Wu Hsin that the understanding depends
But on the listener.
Although one makes no effort to hear,
One must exert great effort to listen.

If you are not listening to Wu Hsin,
What you hear doesn't matter.
If you listen correctly, everything will happen.
Therefore keep questioning to a minimum:
Just listen.

The truth learned from Wu Hsin is of no value;
The only truth which is of value, is the truth which
You have discovered and verified for yourself.

Wu Hsin opens the door;
You must step inside and examine the terrain.

Here, one sets all distractions aside.
Close the eyes and then cover them with cloth.
The removal of the visual removes much of the distraction.

When one's view is that whatever has arisen
Has a role to play,

One need not discriminate and is able to enjoy.
In this context, Wu Hsin has only two requirements.
First, it is important that one acknowledge
The difficulty of seeing beyond
One's ordinary, taken-for-granted perspective and second,
One makes a firm commitment to do so.

Now, understand that
The background assumption of every moment is that
There is something, somewhere, better than
This, here, now.

As such, one becomes deeply habituated to
The unconscious process of constantly
Dislocating from this, here, now.

The most powerful tool at your disposal is doubt.
Doubt every closely held belief, every ontological certitude,
Also doubt Wu Hsin.

Wu Hsin assures you that
No bodily experience can irrevocably
Free you from bodily experience.
Likewise, attention to the mind cannot
Liberate attention from mind itself.

Understand appearance; it is supported by the Real
But it is not real.
It is a seeming reality.
Taking the seeming for the real results in confusion.

Wu Hsin says you are confused because
You have assigned subjectivity to an object.
To you, there is a personal consciousness and
There is everything else that
This consciousness is conscious of.

It should be obvious that everything
Arising out of this errancy mode must
Likewise reinforce confusion.

Now, let Wu Hsin set the backdrop for you.
Life is brief and you are like koi in an evaporating pond.
The outcome is already known.
How your time is spent is what is key.

Wu Hsin grants you only a few questions today, Xu Fengqin.
What are they?

First, Master Wu Hsin, why do you insist on individual instruction?
Is not what is said in the Great Hall sufficient?

The answers to another's questions are often for
That person in that state at that moment only, and
Not necessarily to be applied as general counsel
To anyone else at any time.
Therefore, if you want Wu Hsin's advice, sit here.

Wu Hsin is like a walking stick.
The stick never walks for you;
It walks beside you, assisting you.
Enlightenment is like cleaning a soiled shirt.
Nothing is added to the shirt;
Only the dirt is removed.
The dirt in this case is confusion for which
Doubt and investigation are the cure.

Doubt provides the impetus to investigate.
What is investigated?
The certainty of one's certainty is investigated and thoroughly examined.

If enlightenment occurs,

It will be your unique enlightenment.
It will not be because of anything
Wu Hsin has done to enlighten you.

Next, what is the fastest way to realization?

Trust Wu Hsin and make his words your way of being.
If you never go too far,
You can never discern how far you can go.

For those who do not understand the word of Wu Hsin,
Many scrolls are required.
For a ripe fruit,
Even the subtlest of breezes is sufficient to make it fall.

Toward what should I direct my searching?

Wu Hsin cannot provide directions
To a town that was never built.
Therefore, stop seeking because
What you are searching for is not
An object and as such
Can never be found.

Then release all techniques and strategies for
Ridding yourself of your self.
They only serve to add momentum to
That which already has too much momentum.

All that remains is to settle into that which is already present,
That which need not be sought or manipulated.
It is an emptying.
Usually, a new idea or concept replaces an older one.
In this sense, nothing has been emptied.

Now go, my son,

Tomorrow we begin in earnest.

Awakening

The Master began:
These deep teachings, transmitted orally, are
Passed on to you and thereby preserved from oblivion.
You will hear them.
Do with them as you will.

Wu Hsin is only yourSelf apprising yourself that
You are confused.
You are not what you seem to be.
Wu Hsin's words are the soap that
Cleans away all such confusion.

That which doesn't exist is
Imagining things that don't exist.
This is confusion.

Any discussion of awakening
Requires that Wu Hsin provide a definition.
It is unselfconsciousness.
It is the "non-difference" between
Subject and object or
When you cease to be
What you seem to be now.

It is an event that renders
The self-centric processes inoperative when it strikes.
It is that which cannot be
Characterized by temporal or causal relations.
Even calling it an event is going too far.
It is not unlike what happens to the space inside a bottle
Once the bottle is broken.

It is an extinguishment,
Wherein the fire of self-centricity has gone out
Due to a lack of fuel.
It is the overcoming of all conditioning,
The retracement of I-am-this back through
I-am to I.

The Energy is in a perpetual state of flow.
Self-liberation arrives solely through
The formless practice of non-interference with said flow.
It is a technique-free natural immersion
From which no one returns
Resulting in the unbroken seeing of one's self
Without the aid of a mirror.

It is less a discovery and more of an uncovering.
Your true nature is uncovered when
You remove all the falsity you've heaped upon it.

It is the direct knowledge of yourself as you truly are.

It is the immediate apperception of the truth of things
Without reasoning or analysis;
Immediate knowledge in contrast with
Mediate or indirect, dependent knowledge.

There is an irreversible transformation from
Alone to All-One.
As it is everything and as it is nothing,
It is beyond description.

How will I be changed?

For some but not all,
There is a clear and defined somatic component to it.

In some cases, to outward appearances,
There are no changes.
In others, the changes are subtle while in some,
The changes are more pronounced.
All experience a shift in
The mode of cognition and the frame of reference.
Some require time to stabilize in it;
Others do not.

It is a revelation insofar as what had been veiled is revealed.
It is not so much an awakening as a re-awakening.
It is the realization that the universe is not external to you and
At the same time, it is experiencing that universe as yourself.
It is a realization which transcends philosophy,
A realization that the center is truly everywhere.

It is the perception of the world absent any self-centric filter,
The clear discernment of the underlying unity present in multiplicity.
It is the total, final and absolute dissolution of
The self-obsession, the end of the conceptual entity.

Is it death?

Only in a conceptual sense.
It is more like a location,
That point in time and space where
The idea *I-am-this* used to be.
It is from where no one returns.
It is the cessation of all attachment to phenomena.

It cannot be manipulated into being.
It is an ontic experience,
Something which springs from the center of one's being.
It is the discovery of the infinity which is
At the source of seeming finitude,

Of That which survives all the creations,
All the dissolutions,
That which has no concern for psychological continuity,
Out of which the not yet unfolded,
Not yet finitized, emanates.

Is it what you have called 'clear seeing'?

Yes, it is the seeing of all things in the Self and
The Self in all things.
It is the reconciliation of
The seeming dichotomy of self and not-self.
It is a process of disassembly and reassembly that
Occurs in an instant.

You may still believe that it is within your power
To bring about Self Realization.
The natural consequence of the release of that belief is surrender.

What must become clear is that
The self-referential structure has no trust.
That is why control is so vital to it.
With trust, there is no need for control.

What is required is
The cessation of superimpositions of imagination
Onto What-Is to be replaced by
A communion with It.

What-Is is self regulating, self-fulfilling, s
Self-evolving and self-sustaining.
It needs the help of no outside agency, including yourself.
This reality can never be discerned
Through the prism of self-absorption.

What Wu Hsin is talking about is

The transition from self-reliance to Self-reliance.

So, what is it that can be surrendered?
"I know" can be surrendered,
Individuality can be surrendered
Likewise, the expectation of payoffs for actions.

The latter is why most spiritual practices
Yield incomplete or partial results;
They are motivated by gain, by an ambition

Weather comes and goes
While the sky remains unaffected.
Likewise, space is unaffected by what fills it.

Enlightenment means no longer identifying with the weather.
The particular has been replaced by the universal.

Enlightenment is the undoing of the work of the intellect,
The creation of a self-centric point of reference.
When the center is gone,
The circumference dissolves.
One is without boundaries, everything,
Both the essence and the substance of all that there is.

It is the end of limitation.
It is the recognition of Being,
Of Consciousness, and of Fullness.

Master, is this the natural state?

It is the penetration of those processes
Which frame all the conscious events that appear, all experience.
The re-cognition of what is always already.

To live in one's innate nature is to live naturally.

One need look no further than the animal kingdom
For models of the natural state.
Xu Fengqin, you have been given quite a lot to ponder.
Return to your quarters now and
Consider all that you have heard.

Self Reference

On the twentieth day of the tenth moon,
Xu Fengqin joined the Master after
The day's last meal in the coolness of the garden.
The Master began:

Son, what is at stake in your coming to Wu Hsin?
The existence of the very thing that is questioning,
The questioner, is at stake.
Nothing worldly can satisfy your longing for permanent beatitude.

Man spends his entire life on self-improvement,
On attempting to reconstruct his sense of self whereas
What is really needed is a deconstruction of this sense.
You see, there is always something uncomfortable about it.

This dissatisfaction is the recognition of
The hollowness of the construction:
A mere representation that is friendly to
The society, the language, and need to identify.
It is a product of mental conditioning,
Of an identification with what is limited.

A self requires the support of
Specific referents such as *I, me, mine, myself*.
These words create the illusion that
There must be some thing real that is being referred to.
An image persists because feelings, intentions, and actions
Refer back to it.

Identification is an escape from

The underlying sense of no-thingness.
This attachment conveys a subtle sense of some-thingness.
The more you are identified,
The more you cling to identification.

Self-centricity is therefore a process,
Not a separate entity that exists
Inside the body like a caged animal.

Understand the body as a network of processes.
The response to external situations is
Spontaneous, intuitional, and quite often mechanical,
Without the slightest interference from any seeming individual.

You see Xu Fengqin,
You have imagined a subjectified object and named it 'me'.
It is like mistakenly identifying with
The theatre in which the performance occurs.

This body that you refer to as 'my body' is not yours;
It is a host-body.
You are its guest.
Dead is the condition of this host-body
After the guest departs.

To clarify and resolve
The seeming two-ness in 'me and my body' is sufficient unto itself.
Then, even though one sees all things,
There is not the slightest thread of attachment to them.

What separates is the singular thought: 'I am this'.
Self-consciousness arose and constructed
A seeming individual separate from the world.

Then, what am I?

The sense 'I am' points to an address, a where to seek,
But not any what to seek; and the paradox is that
The "what" cannot be found as an object.
Yet, I somehow always return to the "what".

When the body is fatigued,
One says "I feel tired".
What is it that knows the fatigue?
It can't be the body.
That would be like the tongue discerning
What the mouth tastes like.

There is the total functioning of consciousness
Within the manifestation.
There are no individuals,
Only billions of forms through which the functioning occurs.
The totality is constant,
While the functioning parts come and go.

Whatever one is, must be present always.
All else are added on,
The "what I am" added to the "I am".

When you are sleeping deeply, without any dreams,
You are not associated with your body or your mind.
Who or what is this "you" that is not associated?
This investigation is about removing one's acquisitions so that
All one is left with is what one arrived with.

The core of everything Wu Hsin says, has said, or can ever say,
Can be condensed to this:
Before anything can come into being
There must be some thing to which it comes.
This is the background obscured by the foreground,
The "what".

The world does not exist apart from the body;
Nor the body apart from the mind;
Nor the mind apart from Consciousness;
Nor Consciousness apart from Pure Potentiality.
All is One.

Ponder this until it becomes clear to you that
You are not in pursuit of the Unknown;
You are in pursuit of the Unknowable.

It cannot be perceived.
It cannot even be accurately conceived.
As soon as Wu Hsin attempts to describe It,
He has already soiled It.

To discern what you are,
You must remove those things that constitute your property;
You cannot be your possessions.
These include, your body, your mind, your intellect,
Your feelings and opinions, all material property and
All roles that you have assumed.

What then remains?

You are and you know that you are.
Knowing Presence remains.

With birth, three states begin to cycle and function.
They are the non-experiential state of deep sleep,
The experiential state of waking and dream and
Knowingness Itself.
The first two appear on the third.

Lucid clarity is not something that you have to bring about.
It is what already is

But has been overlooked.
Attention, peace, and silence seem to have been lost
When one becomes otherwise engaged.
Merely check and see if it is really so.

All there is is this Energy and
The functioning of Its manifestation.
Any movement away from that is veering off course.
Wu Hsin cannot stress this enough.
If this is all that you take away from our time together,
It is sufficient.

Everything else: every "me" and every other than "me",
Every second and third person pronoun, is
A mental exercise to bring a sense of order,
Via the creation of narratives,
To all the information that is coming in.

Foremost, this alter-Self is the usurpation of subjectivity.
It assigns reality to itself and
Thereby projects reality onto its perception of the world.

The data from the five senses,
Filtered through the sixth sense which is mind,
Produces the individual's world.

The objects are therefore what one makes of them.
They have no existence independent of the subject.
It is the subjective that requires further examination.
All preoccupation with phenomena is only distraction.

The world is assumed to be real solely because
It appears to be real.
The reflection in the lake is an appearance;
Whatever appears does not affect the lake.

It is only when one turns toward the subject of experience that
One can leave the experienced.
If I know that there is no self, is that enough?

No, knowing there is no self is partial.
That's knowing what isn't without knowing what is.
Intuit what you are.
See that whatever you are must be always present.
You cannot be lost.
Examine your own experience and eliminate the changeful.
You remain.

Real Looking does not involve the mind.
You are present before thought appears,
As that to whom thought arises, and
As that which is aware of thought.
How can the mind look into that which is prior to itself?

Recognize what never changes.
That is the primary re-directing of attention.
See for yourself what your nature is.
Find out based on your own direct investigation,
Not on Wu Hsin's saying it is so.

The one fact you are sure of is that you exist.
Probe into this sense of being that is with you;
Explore for yourself what this Being actually is.

The essential question is one in which
One asks how to be free from
The self-created, self-sustained drama of life and
Its inevitable round of pleasures, confrontations,
Of doubts, searches, and always temporary solutions.

All conventional human pursuits are
A bewildered search based on consensus models of

How things ought to be.
How can you possibly avoid conflict
When you have already established yourself as
The Opponent of all opponents?

The first step is to see that the self has set itself
In opposition to the functioning of the Totality.

And this is where we will leave off for this day, my son.

Wu Hsin will be brief today, Xu Fengqin.
Since the body is in the mind,
It is timely to initiate a regressive look into
The nature of experiencing.

What is it, Xu Fengqin, that experiences?

Master, it is my body that experiences.

By saying 'my body',
A distinction is made between me and the body.
I am I, and the body is mine.
I am not limited by the body;
It is in me.

Begin by removing 'this' from I-am-this.
See that there is no entity there,
Only a distinct, individualized expression of
The Wholeness from which it has emanated,
The vehicle for Experiencing.

Xu Fengqin, what experiences the body?

The mind experiences the body.

What experiences the mind?

(hesitation)

That which sources the mind experiences it. Is that clear?

Yes, Master.

What experiences the source of the mind?

(hesitation again)

The First Cause,
That by which all comes into being,
Experiences the source of the mind.

Drop all ideations of a separate individual.
People are so entrenched in this belief that
They even want it to continue after the body dies.

A sense of embodiment is critical to
A person's notion of self.
Embodiment is the understanding of
The physical body and its relation to oneself.

The sense of who you are is primarily
An identification with the body, the personality,
With its mental processing,
With accompanying emotional investment.

Acting to further extend this experience of "I" is
An overall self-reference whereby
All the "my's" and "mines" provide definition.

However, how can you remain the same over time,
Even as you change, sometimes considerably?

There is no thing or part of you which contains your essence.
Your body, your mind and your memories are
All very important for who you are,
But none of these is the core in which
Your essential identity resides.

Whatever you are made from,
It is the same kind as that of which
Everything else is made of.
Wu Hsin calls it Consciousness.
This is not any personal consciousness,

But the primary building block and support of all things.
If there is no single thing which makes you the person you are,
You must be the result of
Several parts or things working together.

Your sense of self is therefore a construction.

The nature of the self-obsession or alter-Self is
Comprised of three distinct aspects:
First, there is 'I' as the referential center.
It is the core, the entity, the seeming person, the individual.

Next, there is 'me'.
Me is the recipient;
Things happen to it.
It is vulnerable.
It can be harmed and, as such,
It must protect itself by all means necessary.

Last is 'mine'.
It is the further extension of self.
It possesses and therefore
Further defines itself via its possessions.

It is grasping;
It is attachment to objects.
This is its outer realm.
It likewise has an inner realm made up of
Its vehemently held opinions and habituations.

The three aspects enmesh forming a tight composite,
Each complementing the other.
Mine points to 'me' and 'me' refers back to I.

Personal identity is an ever shifting self-image.
No identity is steady and your knowledge about yourself is

Valid only for that moment.

The end result is the axis around which
The rest of the world turns.
However, if it is only a construction,
Can it even be real?

My child, accepting that
The self is an illusion is difficult for most.
The alter-Self seems so convincing, so real.

Ultimately, that which had been limited
Returns to the Unlimited.
Your dissatisfaction with this life prompts you to
Create the concept of next life or afterlife.

Wu Hsin here asserts: when you end, your world ends.

Time-and-space-based Consciousness is
The medium through which
The emanation from the Absolute is
Known, witnessed and experienced.

As an instrument of Consciousness,
The body belongs to Consciousness.
It cannot be 'mine'.

As one gradually withdraws from this sense of ownership,
The body is viewed like a stay in the home of another in that
Nothing there can be referred to as 'mine'.

The alter-Self is actually an impersonal "it."
The problem arises because
One personalizes and identifies with it.
That "it" of the structure is not unique and
It is relatively similar in everyone.

This is the delusion that must be shattered.

Instead of seeing an individual,
The attitude must be
"This is the Energy animating a body,"
Which body answers to Its directions,
As a ship answers to the movements at the helm.

However, adopting this pose is by no means easy.
It conflicts with everything you have been taught
By parents, peers and Chinese society as a whole.

Transcendence or awakening is
The letting go of the identification of a personal self.
The belief in an "I" or "me",
A thing that has its own body, mind, and emotions, is
The sole hindrance to realizing one's true nature.
It is a movement from the fixation of attention on the foreground
Toward attending to the background.

Having heard all this,
Now return to your quarters and
Submit these words to the deepest contemplation.
That will conclude your instruction for today.

Without waiting for Wu Hsin,
Xu Fengqin began the session:

Master, how does the I-am become an individual?

Consciousness is an energy coupling
The existence of knowledge with the knowledge of existence.
When energy manifests through an instrument,
The quality and quantity of said manifestation
Depends on the structure of the instrument.

Sentience is the movement of the energy of consciousness.
There can be no kingdom without a king.
Consciousness is the king and the world its kingdom.
Consciousness is prior to matter,
Essence is prior to substance.

The world does not exist apart from the body;
The body does not exist apart from the mind;
The mind does not exist apart from the Energy; and
The Energy does not exist apart from its Potentiality,
The Absolute.

All there is is the functioning of the manifestation and
The Knowing of the functioning.
It begins with Conscious Being, I.
The verbalized sense of Being is I-am.
This is fullness, unity, peace, with
There being no other to be in conflict with.

Finally, there is the particular experience of being:
I am this.
This is a descent into fragmentation, into limitation.
The experience of being hungry becomes I am hungry.
The experience of being angry becomes I am angry.
The sum of all the particulars becomes

Organized as "me" and its derivative "my".
What can be said to be the obstruction to unity
Other than "other"?
In the instant the "I am this" is born,
The obstruction is set in place.

You meet a woman and fall in love.
You marry.
Five years later, you can't stand her presence.
You see that you only seemed to love her.
You part.
Ten years later, you are now impartial to her presence.
You see that you only seemed to have utter disdain for her.

This is your world,
A series of seeming events,
With this "you" as the central seeming.

When one is clear, when one lets Reality be realized,
It is discerned that
Whatever is mine cannot be 'me' and that
'Me' is nothing other than the particularized experience of That.

What is this That?
It is that by which I-am is known and I am That.
It is achieved via the path of returning.
One returns from what
You have taken yourself to be since
The self-consciousness arose,
When the "I am this" began, to
What was prior to this arising.

This is Wu Hsin's sole instruction:
Go back the way you came.

Wu Hsin has now answered your question for today.

Go and think on this.

Two days hence, Master began his instruction:

What can be known with certainty?

The only thing one can know,
That one can ever know, is
What presents itself in
That consciousness that one essentially is.

A table or a tree exists only
When it appears as a conscious perception.
The only tables and trees that one knows are
Appearances in consciousness.

They arise from the field of consciousness and
Ultimately resolve there.
The appearances change instant by instant, continuously;
The Seeing does not.

Looking inward, what is revealed is that
One is always the silent observing of
Whichever perception presents itself.

All these appear in consciousness,
Like clouds in the sky.
Whether there are big clouds or small clouds,
The silent observing remains itself unchanged.

All phenomena perceived,
The thoughts, feelings and sensations, are
Nothing but movements of energy.

Every movement is in time,
Having its beginning, its crest and its dissolution there.
Consciousness, the Experiencing that you are, is
Present before a movement commences,

Throughout its duration and after its disappearance,
Just as water must be there before the birth of any wave,
Remaining as such during its lifetime, and even after
The wave has disappeared.

Seeking is consciousness seeking its source.
There is no individual.
There is only you,
The total functioning as you.
The total functioning is you.
The consciousness is you.

Every moment the attention is going outward toward the world.
Were it redirected inward and
Were it to stabilize there,
All your problems would dissolve.

Wu Hsin invites you to see for yourself.
Unfortunately, most people don't understand Wu Hsin.

They cannot understand because they
Process his words through the known.
The known can never go beyond itself and
This "beyond the known" is all that he talks about.

The known has value,
In the same way that a stone has value.
That doesn't mean you have to
Carry it with you at all times.

What must be seen is that
This collection of world, body, mind and Energy
Comprise a single unity.

However, it is within the fundamental nature of mind
To create duality, I and other.

It is the maker of "many".

If you dream of an elephant,
The elephant appears vividly in full detail.
But when you wake up,
You realize that it was just an appearance in the mind.
You don't wonder 'Where is the elephant now?', because
You understand that it was only a projection and
Had no existence outside your mind.

When the awareness that apprehended the elephant ceased,
The elephant did not go anywhere,
It simply disappeared, for it was just
An appearance to the mind and
Did not exist separately from the mind.

Likewise, the entirety of the gross world
Emerges from the mental plane.
When it is analyzed, it is found to exist inseparably from it.

You have to see that
Every projection of a "you" is a movement away from yourself.
You erect a wall around yourself through
The self-referential thoughts 'I', 'me' and the 'mine'.
Yet, it is only in fact memory;
In its absence, who are you?

It manifests as three types of desires:
Relationships, possessions, and affirmation.
It is the drive to be powerful and relevant.
It is a moving target,
Constantly changing its center of identification.
One minute, it is identified with outside things,
Next moment with the body,
Then with the senses or thoughts.

What is lost is the remembrance that
You are the Great Essence,
The basis of all things.

Starve the I-thought by
Depriving it of all other thoughts and perceptions that
It normally identifies with.

It is the cessation of the label "mine".
When the self-fixation on 'I', 'me' and the 'mine' is released,
"True-I" is revealed.

There are no techniques, no practices, other than
Formless practice.
What you really are is never achieved through technique.
Technique is movement away from it.

See that to live as a person is to live a life of restriction.
Each person has to be a certain way,
In those modes of behavior that define that person.

This illusion of individuality is the source of all other illusions.
It is a learned response, a reflex.
When the habit is broken,
Interest wanes in the source illusion and clarity pervades.

When you free yourself from your concepts and conditioning,
You live in the beauty of your absence,
In the absence of any one in particular.

Does this mean that I am seeing incorrectly; is this so?

Ordinary appearances represent
A fundamental misperception of Reality wherein wakefulness is
An imaginative state fed by sense perception, and
Dreaming is another imaginative state

Sheltered from sense perception and fed by memory.
These two constitute the experiential state
Which is no different from individual mind.

Such an individual mind is
The imagination that there is an independent self.
It is the seed from which
The entire self-narrative grows and is
The underlying cause of the
Straying away from presence.

Seeming self is an energetic spasm or flux
That occurs at a precise moment in
The development of intellect.
It is the reaction to the misperception of
A seeming separation from Source.

The alter-self is the body as object.
Within this framework,
One considers one's presence only as
A phenomenon when the body was there.

Whereas inauthentic or alter-I is
The pseudo-subject of awareness,
'Me' is the object of awareness, and 'mine' are its attachments.
It is like iron coinage, of importance only as long as
You believe in its value.

The answer to 'Who am I?' is no body.
No body points to that which is without form.
Formlessness is my form.
I am intangible;
I am full and I am empty.
Nothing can be added to me
Nor can anything be taken away.

Objects can be differentiated by means of their forms,
But I am always undifferentiated I.

Wu Hsin has nothing more to say.

The Energy

Today, Xu Fengqin, Wu Hsin shall expound further
On consciousness and on the Energy.

Every utterance of 'I' is to be understood to be
The voice of the Energy and every 'me' Its object.

The Energy is that by which 'this' is illuminated.
As It works in humans,
It produces a world representation.
Having a body is Its descent into form from the Primal Field.

In Its absence, how could any action occur?
It is the medium for access,
For perceiving and experiencing the world.
The thought "I am" is the world; it contains the entire world.
Once there is acknowledgement that you are, the world is there.

Personal consciousness takes this medium hostage and
Creates a self-referential center through which
The entirety of the perceived and the experienced can be framed,
A point of view.
Attention is the selectivity of this personal consciousness.

Is it the Witness?

The world, as it is, is infinite and eternal.
It is all Now and Here.
However, Consciousness is "of something" and "as something".

When one seeks to examine the observer among the observed,
One discerns that the organism observing is just another object.

It cannot be the subject.
When no true subject can be found,
One can conclude that the observer and the observed are not
The dyad that they seemed.

The subject can't be found because
The subject is everywhere, like air.
How do you find air?

To embrace the Energy is to
Embrace the player of the music,
Not its instrument,
Not its sounds.

Only when the mind is not translating what it hears
In terms of what it knows can insight arise.
Theories are many and
They can provide much in the way of intellectual entertainment.

However, you have come here not to
Massage your ambition for gain,
Not to debate various theories endlessly,
But to recognize What-Is and to recognize It today.

So, let us face the matter together, my child.

One must recognize the limitations of words.
Wu Hsin is like a mute
Trying to communicate what sweet melon tastes like.
The Ground is unutterable.
It cannot be described.

What can be said is that
There is something more subtle than this gross body
Which expresses itself via your voice.
Speech is verbalized thought;

Thought is always antecedent to speech.
All speech is the expression of mind,
The sum of thoughts.

What is it that hears these expressions of mind prior to their being spoken, my Master? What is it that perceives?

That which perceives objects cannot be an object itself.
There is a brief experience of it in the morning on waking.
A subtle conscious presence is intuited that is there to
Greet the world.

As the sun doesn't cease to exist at night,
This conscious presence doesn't cease to exist
In the absence of anything to be conscious of.

Energy moving through space creates wind.
The same energy moving through water that creates waves.
That energy moving through the brain creates
Waves of thought.
The totality of thought we call mind.

The waves rise and fall,
Come and go.
The Energy remains.

This Energy uses the seeming individual as its instrument.
This is apperceived when the attention rests
Somewhere other than on thought.
The mind is not the instrument to use to attain true peace.
The mind cannot know true peace, Xu Fengqin, because
The mind is the antithesis of peace.

At best, it may discern an echo of peace,
Nothing more.

When every inch of the scroll is covered with letters,
The background, the scroll, is lost.
This world is one such writing and
It is the mind which both impedes and distorts
Your perception of the scroll.

Can a puppet move without
The strings in the hand that moves it?
One is the embodiment of the Energy.
Hence, one knows one is and
One is conscious of such knowing.

Let us stop here for today.
Give my words your deepest consideration, Xu Fengqin.
They will serve you most well.

The Master picked up from where he left off:
My son, let us now continue
The instruction concerning the Energy.

Consciousness is like space.
Formless, invisible,
It is the support of all that appears.
It is Your instrument;
You use it to come to know and
Experience yourSelf as expressed objectively.

Whereas the Energy performs all the actions,
Consciousness does the observing.

This Consciousness is the light which makes not only darkness
But also light perceivable.
Only under the light of Consciousness can
Darkness remain darkness.

Observing is the natural state.
Observing involved with the observed is experience.
The body is what events happen to while
Observing remains unaffected.

Don't try to go beyond consciousness;
Only stabilize there.
If some need arises to go beyond consciousness,
The appropriate action will arise.

Examine everything.
Observe all observation including
The "observer" who is observing.
Also observe the moment of observation in order to
Discern the origination of observation.

The one who realizes is

One who has examined everything.
By examining, you come to know.

Source and Its Objects

How can Wu Hsin comment upon that where
Words do not reach?
To describe the wordless state requires words.
How accurate can such a description be?

Whatever Wu Hsin may say is
One sentence too many.
People come to him,
Then automatically words emerge.
There is no intention behind it.

All sentient life flows from the same source.
It can be said to be uncreated insofar as
It is not a creation separate from a creator.
It is an emanation,
An objective expression of the Subject.

What is this life other than movement,
Processes within the Energy?
There are no discrete entities, only processes.
No seekers, only seeking;
No thinkers, only thinking.

One can never understand the forest by focusing on the foliage.
For as long as you hold to the notion of distinct identities, my son,
You will remain mired in delusion.

One believes oneself to be that which, in reality,
One is not.
Until this stops,

How can one hope to reach the Ultimate?
Examine how the human organism in its functioning.
Stimulus-response activated, habitual, mechanical,
It is driven for self-preservation and self-perpetuation.

Phenomena perceived are framed by how
They relate to a seeming self-center.
Thus, everything is viewed through
The aperture of individuality.

Your sense of being is without a body.
Even in total sensory deprivation,
You know that you are.

However, you have developed the habit of
Imagining yourself perceivable and describable.
You are separated from the external world insofar as
You take yourself to be a thing
Sensed among other things sensed.
You know your so-called self only
Through the senses and the mind.

Thoughts give form and definition to the body,
Otherwise you have no way of experiencing it.
Thought functions as the seeming protector of continuity:
The body's, the mind's, the person's.

What knowledge does a man, blind since birth,
Have of his body?
The nose cannot smell it;
The tongue cannot taste it,
The ear cannot hear it.
Only the body can touch the body.

That which makes experience possible is the Absolute,
The Father of the Energy.

That which makes it actual is the Energy.
Everything becomes visible because of this which is invisible.
That which is aware that you are talking to yourself
Must be antecedent to that which is talking.
It is That which has its stand outside of time and space.

It is That by which the totality of the universe is experienced,
That which creates both one and two.
That which can be created is
What was not there before.
The Never Not doesn't fit into this category, therefore
It is also referred to as the Uncreated.

The ending begins right after beginning begins.
When the sense I-am goes,
It takes time and space with it.
This re-establishes emptiness.

What is emptiness empty of?

Emptiness is empty of other.

How can it be known?

It is the unseen source of possibility,
In the same way that water makes tea possible.
It is the First Cause in the same way as
Birth is the first cause of death.

To say that the world is an appearance is
An incomplete statement.
The correct statement is
"So-and-so in the world is an appearance".

Why is this significant?
Because it includes the seer as part of the appearance,

The import of which is that
An appearance can't independently do anything.
That which produced the appearances
Controls all the activities that go on in it.

The entire series of appearances is on
The wall that is Mind.
As Consciousness, I am that which illuminates the screen.
Absolutely, I am the source of Consciousness.

All there is is the universal field of transcendent potential,
The Absolute.
It is that from which the Energy emerges,
Enlivening living things, providing sentience to sentient beings.
Like the Absolute,
The Energy cannot be known directly in the sense that
An object can be known.
It can only be known through its effects, perception and action.

However, this natural openness has been
Covered over by intellect and its offspring, self-consciousness.
In that sense, lucidity is not so much
A discovery as an uncovering.

It is a cessation of the old methods of adaptation,
A shift from identification with a body/mind and
Toward identification with what knows it.

There is None Other.
Is It not only experiencing Itself?

One can never find It as long as
It is treated as other.
When there is no other,
There is no need to find anything.
All that is needed is that you come to discern that

There is no 'I' other than Self and
This Self is self-evident.
You know It,
You feel It because
You are It.

There is nothing whatsoever to be done?

One's essential nature,
The innately luminous residing within all beings, is
Already present.
Any path moving toward It actually is
Movement away from It.
No conditioned action can take one to the Unconditioned.

Therefore, Xu Fengqin, all that is required for
Provoking the awareness of the true nature of reality is
The sustaining of an unobstructed view.
This is Wu Hsin's technique-free path,
Passing beyond effort, beyond practice,
Beyond aims and goals.

The recognition of Immanence,
That which is immanent in all phenomena,
Removes the fixation of the attention to appearances.

In so doing,
One transcends one's ordinary, taken-for-granted perspective and is
Thereby naturally and spontaneously present in
A state of immediate, unconditioned awareness,
Being undistracted by either
The outer world of sensations or
The inner world of mentation.

This concludes our time today.

Seated crossed legged on the floor, the Master spoke:

Everyone is clamoring for Self consciousness,
Yet almost none are willing to pay for it.
What is the price of Self-consciousness?
The price of Self-consciousness is self-consciousness.

How can I come to understand Self-consciousness that is different from self-consciousness?

Wu Hsin can take you within sight of it.
But the actual seeing is in your hands, Xu Fengqin.

Consciousness can never be fully known.
One can't stand outside it to examine it and
Any view from inside consciousness is, at best partial.

Consciousness is something one is,
Not something one has.
It is simply 'presence to', 'awareness of'.

Consciousness is the womb of becoming.
Nothing exists in the absence of consciousness.
Consciousness contains everything.
As all tidal waves are inside the ocean,
All worlds are inside consciousness.

All it takes is a single thought.
In the absence of thought,
The foundation and support of all is revealed.

The problem of understanding consciousness is
Understanding who or what experiences consciousness.
It's like a ring;
The center is missing.
Your body appears to you as a series of sensory perceptions.

It is in this way that
You know you have a body,
When you feel it.
These perceptions appear to you,
Pure conscious attention.

Wu Hsin has told you before that
The Energy is that by which 'this' is illuminated.
In the absence of consciousness,
How could you know anything?
As such, the consciousness aspect of the Energy is
Antecedent to all knowing.
In every moment, it is selecting one out of
The thousands of possible interpretations of the apparent world.

Consciousness is the medium for access,
For perceiving and experiencing the world.
The thought "I am" is the world;
It contains the entire world.
Once there is acknowledgement that you are,
The world is there.

Personal consciousness creates
A self-referential center through which
The entirety of the perceived and the experienced can be framed,
A point of view.

However, the Energy stays ever in charge.
We see this when a burnt finger retracts from the fire
Much before we become aware of the pain.

What then constitutes the real "you"?
There are no activities of any individual.
There is only the activity of
The Unmanifest as manifestation.

Self-conscious senses the emptiness of the self.
It comes to fear the emptiness.
In so doing, there is an outward movement to
Fill that nothing with something to mitigate the fear.

In this way, the processes of acquiring and becoming begin.
Rigorous observation of the so-called person is
Sufficient to undo this.
You will see that it is merely a construction.

However, be warned Xu Fengqin.
This not a cognitive exercise to be performed intellectually.
You go in and have a look around.
Wu Hsin can provide you with the key,
But if you keep it in your pocket,
The door will never open.

Therefore, make a clear distinction between
Thinking and knowing.
What is thinking other than the layering of concepts?

The primary concepts, Xu Fengqin, are:
I am this person, in this body,
Acting in this world
Able to discern between polarities
Such as good and bad,
Right and wrong.

These primary concepts are not questioned,
Taken to be absolute.
Everyone is lazy.
No one demands proofs,
No one investigates.
Because one merely accepts what one is told,
One is deeply conditioned.

The body is taken as real but
One only knows the body through
The senses of the body.

If you lose bits of your body,
An arm or a leg,
Your friends will still recognize you.

No one's words, including Wu Hsin's,
Can take you to That which is prior to words.
Any truth that can be spoken cannot be the Truth.
The best Wu Hsin can do is to point out the false as false.

Your days here are
An opportunity to look at what is there in
The absence of thought,
What is independent of thought.

When the attention is moved elsewhere,
There is no preoccupation with thought.
As you are not moment-to-moment conscious of your breathing,
The same can apply to thought.

Suddenly, without this self-consciousness,
The world is transformed.
A peaceful calm is apperceived.

Day-to-day perception is relative and objective,
It is perceiving how one object relates to another.
This type of perception is impure and requires conception,
The establishment of concepts.

That is where the mind function comes in to play.
Your present confusion is that
You have identified with the picture, the image and not with
That onto which it appears,

To which it comes.

This point is quite subtle and therefore seems elusive.
Your own changelessness is so obvious that
You don't notice it.
Regardless of the cataclysms that may appear,
That one which they appear is unaffected.

One then lives like an animal,
Attending neither to what may be nor
To what has been, perpetually present.
He is not bound by 'do's' and 'don't's'.
He lives an unintentional life wherein
Things go on normally and
Nothing is resisted.

Effort

Whomsoever It chooses,
To this one,
It reveals Itself.
Therefore, what can be the point of effort and will?
Effort and willing are only sources of stress.

Reality is unconditioned,
While practices and techniques must, by their definition,
Conceal Reality as they are movements away from It.

This Reality that does not exclude confusion;
Seeing through the confusion is Reality.

Master, how can anything be attained without effort?

There are some things which effort cannot produce.
Can effort make one beautiful?

So what is your advice?

Wu Hsin advises only rest;
Not seeking is resting.

I cannot see myself not making some effort.

If you want to make any effort,
Why not try to dis-identify from
The one making the effort?

Just as the viewer cannot be found in that which is viewed,
To search for yourself externally is like

Trying to capture the wind.
When the energy that is spent in
The pursuit of something that does not exist,
Perpetual continuity, is freed up,
Then the goal no longer seeds the search.

What effort is required to experience the world?
The same amount of effort is required to experience yourSelf,
Once the experiencing of the world is no longer the priority.
As such, Xu Fengqin,
Rearrange your priorities.

Master, what is it that I must renounce as the price for this?

Your mistaken ideas regarding renunciation only
Create more fantasies.
Giving up a thing for a better one is not renunciation.
Nor is true renunciation rejection as much as it is impartiality.
With conventional renunciation,
Rejection has not been renounced.

To some, this may sound like too lofty a task.
If that is the case,
Begin by admitting your inability to
Produce your intended outcome and
Simply renounce your agenda.

Suffice it to say that all your troubles began when
You decided to become an individual.
It must become clear that
Whatever you are doing to
Free yourself from the self is that self itself.

This, by necessity, must therefore
Negate any idea of how-to.
As soon as you ask "how to?",

You have already conceived that
There is some problem requiring solution and then
You set out to seek said solution.

All seeking, even spiritual seeking, is
The seeking of advantage.
But Wu Hsin tells you that
All of your attempts to manipulate What-Is
So that it better suits you
Will provide only temporary respite at best.

You accept the idea that there is something to change,
Yet you never question the existence of
The one who is to be changed.
There is no personal transformation,
Only transformation away from the personal.

When you want something,
Normally you know what needs to be done to get it.
But what if the wanted is non-objective,
Prior to the subject-object structure?

What method will enable you to attain an end
Which is impossible to attain?
If you make no effort,
There can be no result or even progress.
But to the extent that you exert yourself to attain it,
You fail.
This is the paradox.

Any method assumed to lead to enlightenment presupposes
The cause/effect dualism that it strives to escape.
Any technique to escape the throes of the narrative are
Part of the narrative.
All effort reflects the desire to exercise control over a process.
It is self-delusion that effort solves everything.

When you scraped your knee as a child,
What effort did you make to heal it?
When you desired to grow taller,
What effort did you make?

The same effort that was
Required for you to grow physically is also
Necessary for you to grow consciously.

Stop using this moment to get somewhere else.
Bring an end to this strategy of ceaseless becoming.

This form is in the service of Consciousness.
Yes, Wu Hsin appears to perceive, speak and act,
But it just happens,
In the same way that he perspires.
There is neither a conscious decision
Nor a conscious decision maker.

From the moment one wakes up
Until one falls asleep,
One is very busy doing something.
What vitalizes this doing,
What is its motive force?

It is the Energy.
Understand that the Energy will see to it that
All of your needs will be met.
Likewise, understand that it is not
The responsibility of this same Energy to fulfill your wants.

Set your sights on that which is invisible.
Once this is firmly in place,
When that which is visible arises,
It will be clearly understood.

Then, there is no viable path to enlightenment?

A viable path should be like a recipe;
You follow the instructions and
You get the results.

Those defending paths and
The failures that occur in them will, as a rule,
Fault the application by the practitioner,
The impurities of the practitioner or
The capacity of the practitioner.
But this is all mere conjecture.

To admit to oneself that one is totally confused is
The beginning of real understanding.
"You" requires localization.
You are in this world when awake and in
Another world in your dreams.
In the absence of locale,
The "you" is not.

What is everywhere cannot have a location;
It is in the worldly realm.
Such is the case with the Energy.

Having a body and a brain is inadequate for perceiving.
Corpses meet this qualification
Yet they do not perceive.
The support of perceiving is this Energy and
It experiences itself through its localization in a body.

The sense of "I" pertains to the body.
"Me" is only the I-thought made material and
The world is the other-than-I thought made material.

The outward perspective is mandated by
The organism's instinct for survival.
It is perpetually scanning the landscape.
To redirect one's attention inward goes against
The most basic of drives.

You have always been exercising your intellect and
Never your intuition.
If you reverse course and look inward,
Shutting out all external images and
Falling back on intuitive feeling,
You will receive the true picture of yourself.

This is the real and
The realization of the One which words cannot describe,
Which the mind cannot reach, and
Which is merely suggested by any term.

If one keeps the attention fixed on the sense of 'I' and
By remaining there,
The seeming self loses its hold.

Attending to Self is nothing but abiding as Self.
It is not doing,
But being.
It is not a mental activity
But your natural state of existence.

Xu Fengqin, keep in mind
Intellectual analysis cannot provide the necessary understanding.
But if you take note of the clues,
With experiment and experience,
The true understanding dawns when
You rest in that state of Self-abidance.

Peace of mind cannot be obtained;
Peace of mind is
The antithesis of peace.
Mind cannot be permanently made peaceful.

A self trying to develop selflessness is
Like extinguishing a lamp with lamp oil.
The self cannot dissolve itself;
Only the Self can dissolve the self.
One must only stand vigilant.

Why do you say to stand vigilant?

Vigilance purifies the mind.
To stand apart from the mind and watch its activities,
This moment of disassociation, is
An instantaneous, albeit momentary, dissolution of the mind.

Give up all preconceived notions and ideas taken from others,
Wu Hsin included.
See for yourself.
Understand for yourself.
Only in this fashion can realization,
This spontaneous intuition, be truly yours.

You have to make a commitment.
When you decide to stop settling for what is temporary,
The world loses its appeal, Xu Fengqin.
Commit to the permanent, the unchanging.

You can only identify with something perceivable, an object.
You are subjectivity itself, non-objective,
The center out of which perception arises.
Identification with any thing is always an error.
See your error and be done with it.

It is Wu Hsin's experience that
Most people come here to gather information.
They have the mistaken notion that information equates with knowledge.
They then take that information and treat it like
Something to be stored away.
This is the wrong approach.

Everyone thinks that their view or their path is right.
When you accept "what seems to be" as "what is",
Then you remove the possibility of
The need for investigation.

One must concede that the way in which things appear is
Causally determined by a number of factors which are
Extraneous to the thing itself.
The words "outer" and "inner" relate to the body only.
In reality, the outer is merely a projection of the inner.
They are one.

There is no non-dual manifestation.
Manifestation is duality,
A movement from the causal,
Through the subtle, to the gross.
In this manner, daily life cycles from
The dreamless void, to dream, to waking in the world.

Begin by understanding the problem;
Let us not first concern ourselves with action,
With what to do.

What part of you can claim to be
Unchangeable, independent, and autonomous?
You are constantly changing, ever-moving.

Were you born?

Birth can't be remembered.
Is there any difference between
I don't remember and I don't know?

Too, although dying can be known,
Death cannot be known.
Existence is defined between these two unknown points.

Wu Hsin can tell you that
You were born with the Universe and
When you end, it likewise ends,
Your having no evidence to the contrary.

But this is limited existence,
Defined by those two points.
Can there be an unlimited existence,
Without beginning, without end?
Wu Hsin declares that there can be.

How then to move beyond the limited existence?
Can the self free itself from itself?
This is the problem you are faced with.

All aspiration must involve cutting through confusion and,
In so doing, unveils the awakened, natural or essential.
However, were recognition to be the product of practice,
Then it contains an inherent dependency,
Being a result of cause and effect.
If it is caused, it may later become uncaused.

However, true recognition is permanent because
One has not produced it;
One has merely re-discovered it.

The observation "There is pain" is prior to
The expression "I am in pain".

Somewhere in between the observation and the expression,
"I" is introduced.
Who is it, or what is it, that
Introduces this "I"?

Can one draw any distinction between
The body in the world and
The conceptual "me"?
Can one kindle an awakening to
The everpresent, unchanging Energy?

Wu Hsin suggests it is indeed possible
Via an inquiry into the nature of
A consciousness that is present
Even when one is unconscious.

In order that they can be referenced,
Forms require names.
Prior to receiving a name and
Knowing oneself to be the name relating to the form,
One did not know oneself.
It is not prior to consciousness
But it is prior to self-consciousness.

When the body awakens in the morning,
The world awakens with it.
Perceived by the senses, this totality seems real.
But this body in this world is temporal, transitory.
It comes, it goes.

That which knows all comings and goings stands outside them.
There is no thing independent of It.
This is where the attention should be fixed.

All practices have to fail because
They are responses by separative selves to

The original premise of substantive self-existence.
That assumed view is a matter of
Uninspected convention, unproven belief.

Is there any practice that doesn't reinforce the idea "I am this".
Can you extinguish a fire with cooking oil?

It is only when the commitment to the Self is
Stronger than the commitment to distraction that
Any positive movement can be claimed.

In the beginning, there must come about
A rejection of the mechanical way of being
That is replaced by a submission to, and
A communion with, one's Source.

As this strengthens,
There is then a movement closer to the natural state.
In any moment, you can declare
"I submit, I yield, I submit".
This is the submission of the self to the Self.

How can I not be involved?

Tremendously complex processes are going on
All the time in you.
None of them require your involvement.

What is called life consists of the organism's efforts to
Ensure its self-preservation and self-replication.

What you call "my life" is
The narrative that is constructed surrounding
The so-called person's interactions with "other" and
The attempts at fulfilling personal wants.

The person then takes on the drives of the organism
To perpetuate itself and to replicate itself.
This is done by forming attachments to things which
Serve as extensions of oneself: mine.
The sum of these extensions,
The totality of "mine" equals the self.

The self is really a construction of the imagination,
Something created to account for the multiplicity of
Sensory impressions, emotions, thoughts, and feelings that
Come continuously.

You are a point in space and time from which
A manifested world is experienced.
This is the starting point for the investigation:
"What is experiencing the world?"
You can only experience rafting the river by being
Attached to the raft.
All experience requires attachment.

Observing is of two types.
The first is without involvement and is referred to as witnessing.
The second is with involvement or attachment and is
Referred to as "my life".

Seek out from where the world emanates in
The same way as one relentlessly searches from where
A foul odor emanates.

Xu Fengqin, these are the specifics of your investigation:

Can you sense that you are and that
You know that you are?

Did you have to do anything to acquire that sense "I am"?

Do you need to make an effort to access or sustain it?
Can you stop the sense of this aware presence?

Does it have a unique location?

Does it have a beginning or an end?

Does it have preferences?

Has it aged as you have?

Is it something you have, is it your awareness or
Is it only awareness?

Do any sensory perceptions, thoughts, memories, and imaginations exist independent of it?

Is it separate from you?

Is it the same as mind or
Is it that which knows the contents of the mind?

Can this sense of aware presence be described?

Is it intermittent; does it come and go?

Do you need a practice or a special technique to
Recognize this being-awareness?

Does seeing it require meditation,
An awakening or some other spiritual experience?

When the sensing is not clear and obvious,
What obscures it from you?

Wu Hsin trusts that these will suffice.

Let us reconvene in two days hence.

Xu Fengqin, today we will discuss conviction.

To reach conviction about anything is possible in two ways.
You either have full faith in the words that have come to you or
You rigorously, unflinchingly perform your own investigation.
The former is quicker whereas the latter takes more time.

Many come to Wu Hsin as
Individuals expecting to get something,
But they remain ill-prepared for the getting.
They are like a blind man who
Wants to be taught how to paint.
Those who want to investigate and examine must
Establish the primacy of consciousness.
Then, inspect the previously uninspected identification of consciousness with phenomena.

You burn your garbage.
You die so that you never have to die again.
Then you get to meet yourself in the way that
The face meets its image in the reflective surface.

You simply abide in and as Radiant Being.

Let us pause for a few hours.
Retire to your quarters and begin to plant those seeds that will result
The fruits of conviction.

In the afternoon session, Master Wu Hsin began:

Whatever Wu Hsin says is either
Accepted or rejected based on your frame of reference.
It is mere interpretation.
What happens if the frame of reference goes?
What happens if the person is no more?

Self-born clarity or Self-realization is
The discovery by yourself that
There is no separate self to be discovered.
It is a reversion to true nature.

There is no entity.
There is subjective functioning, process.
There is no witness, only Witnessing or Observing.

Being aware of aware being
Equals 'I am'.
In that, there is the potential to observe.
This is discerned as two aspects:
Conscious being observes phenomena while
The Absolute observes conscious being.
In this manner,
The Subject comes to know Itself.

Is the seeing of this enlightenment?

Since What-Is is unconditioned Transcendent At-One-Ment,
All forms of duality represent a distortion of What-Is.
Thus, confusion is birthed,
Confusion being the entanglement of Primordial Being with
The dichotomizing, obscuring qualities of mentation.

What must be done to make muddy water clear?
Only let it be.

In time, it clears itself.

In the absence of activity,
The source and support of all activity can be recognized.
Beyond body-consciousness though embodied,
One directly sees that which sees and
Thereby is Self-realized.

Nothing need be suppressed;
Only don't fixate attention.
This results in the uninvolved observation of
The functioning of the totality.
Phenomena no longer affect you in the same way that
Smoke doesn't affect the sky.

Experience

The Master began his instruction today:
The Energy is the basis of all experience.
It is the witness and support of them all.

Within experience, three states continuously cycle in man.
Each one is exclusive of the other two and defined by
The conditions of time and space.
The three phases of phenomena are
Appearance, continuity and dissolution.

Every moment, there is the experience "I am".
Yet, that which experiences,
Experiencing Itself, remains unidentified.

When both what is and what is not have disappeared
Then what remains is the essence.

Liberation is nothing else than
Seeing this with full conviction.

The instrument of consciousness for observation is attention.
When attention is coupled with involvement,
There is experience.

All too often,
When you pay attention to the object
You forget the substance.

Embodied sentience is the instrument of Experiencing.
The progression begins with embodied sentience,
Then embodied mentation leading to embodied self.

I must be involved with an object to experience it?

Yes, you must know a thing in order to experience it.
First it is observed;
Then it can be experienced.

How is unity experienced?

Where there is only One,
There is no experience because
There is nothing apart from One to be experienced.

Beingness is the pre-verbal 'I am'.
It is presented with two states,
The experiential and the non-experiential.
Just as one side of a coin cannot see the other,
The non-experiential state cannot be had from
The experiential state.

How then can it be attained?

When there is no attachment to phenomena,
There is only witnessing, observing.
Witnessing is awareness of
The movements in consciousness.

This is what has been overlooked.
You can only know what you remember.
You cannot know what you can't remember.

This somebody that you take yourself to be is
Only memory, of past images of yourself.
Unshackle yourself from it.

The past is an artifact of perception

Brought into the present by imperfect memory.
As such, the past is always imperfectly represented.
You are imperfectly representing yourself to yourself.

Focus on the discovery of
What is aware of the sense of existence, of I-ness,
Rather than a projected 'me' standing in for 'I'.

Soon, the idea that the body was ever considered to be 'me'
Will be revealed to be absurd.

You are the awareness of phenomena,
The Observing.
You are the awareness of involvement with phenomena,
The Experiencing.

This true understanding is Self-revealing;
It is not acquired nor is it attained.
It occurs when the obstacles standing in its way are removed.
These obstacles fall of their own accord
When their underpinnings are eliminated.
It is the end of pronouns.

Descriptions of the world are no longer framed in "is" or "are",
But are now referenced with "seems to".

One is knowing oneself at present through the body-form:
With the mind, self-sense, intellect, and so many concepts.
But you are beyond that;
Your Presence is not that.

Everything starts from you and ends in you,
With the paradox being that there is no you.
You are Consciousness Itself.
So you can never separate yourself from That.

You always think 'I exist'.
Every moment your body and mind are changing,
But in the middle of all these changes
The unchangeable notion 'I exist' persists.
You never think 'I don't exist'.
This awareness of 'I exist' is the reflection of the real 'I'.

There is nothing to give up or to get hold of;
What exists always exists.
Only one 'I' exists.

Wu Hsin's advice is simple:
Step out of the field of thought and keep watching.
Who other than you is observing?
You are the Witnessing.

Q: Is witnessing different from seeing?

Before the next thought or image appears,
You are already there, standing ready.
There is no "I", "you", or "other" present there.

Seeing that, being that, will express itself
Simply by being what you are,
Witnessing.

Everything is the Seeing without distinction.
It is only the mind that appears to divide
The natural oneness into
A fragmentary array of things appearing and disappearing.
This is the structure of the human sensory systems.

Man doesn't like to have his world view challenged or
Even brought into question.
One who has nothing to defend can never be offended.
As long as there is something left to defend and

Something with which to resist,
As long as there is something still left to die,
The condition called 'suffering' must persist.

Seeking out new experiences is
Movement in the wrong direction.
Clarifying that which is common to all experience is
The correct way.

Those who have come to Wu Hsin for
New experiences have been misadvised.
You already have all the experience you need.
The past ones are sufficient.

Nor is Wu Hsin here to inspire you.
Lost, desperate people have created
Many religious intermediaries who
Stand ready to provide inspiration.

Only those who genuinely want rest should
Visit Wu Hsin's mountain and listen to him.

World

The Master placed his hand in Xu Fengqin's shoulder and began:

Only a wise man looks at a tree
While never forgetting its root.
All others become fixated on the activities
Occurring in the branches and leaves.

The world is constantly trying to
Shake itself free from your clutches.
Pain, sorrow and dissatisfaction are its tools.
Once it frees itself, the unexpected happens:
Happiness and peace reveals itself.

The more powerfully one looks to the external world,
The more completely one forgets Oneself.

Regardless of the number of species,
Existence, life, is only One.
Yet, every creature has its own world.

The world is the seen.
The seer is the instrument in the world
Via which it is seen.
It is part of the world.
The Seeing is not a thing;
It is the Subjective.

All there is is the world and
The Seeing of it.

What is born is the experiential state,

The non-experiential state and
The consciousness that knows them.

What is the relationship between the Energy and the world?

The Energy and the world are like thread and cloth.
If there is no thread, there is no cloth.

The phenomena that is called 'the world' is
Not separate nor different from That Which Is any more than
Sunlight is different from the sun.

In the process of manifestation,
Three things sequentially emanate:
First time, then space and last, phenomena.
You are that which is prior to them all,
The Knowing of them all.

The ongoing questions over whether or not the world is real
Distracts you from grander pursuits.

All worlds have a conditional reality;
They are real while you are in them and unreal
When you take your stand outside.
That which knows all conditional worlds is
Antecedent to any of them.

What you are is antecedent to
All concepts of what you are.
You stand in pure awareness of the transient as transient, and
The imaginary as imaginary.

You will come to discern that your world is in your mind.
However, to fully know it,
You must be free of all involvement with it.

You can observe the clouds moving across the sky
Without any involvement with them.
All of your so called life should be treated in like manner.

The world continues until the death of the body.
However, the awakened no longer takes the world personally.

I don't have the feeling that world is in my mind. It feels external.

The outer being merely a projection of the inner,
'You in the world' is only a mental construction.

Admittedly, you appear to exist.
Wu Hsin repeats: "appear to exist".

What appears to exist eclipses the Eternal.
The end of the eclipse is the end of confusion,
The end of 'you'.
Until that time,
You'll continue to replace one mode of confusion with another.

That which owns the body likewise owns the world.
Its name is I.
Reflected in the mind, it is I-am.
I-am is the truth whereas
I-am-this is a distortion of it.

The body is the vehicle by which one learns one's existence.
First, there is embodiment.
Then, a few years later, one knows that one is and
Begins to form concepts of what one is.
Here, we re-examine those concepts.

Awakening is the death of individuality.
When the drop is absorbed back into the ocean,
There is no longer any notion of being a drop.

Wu Hsin is helpless to take from you that which
You refuse to part with.
If you insist on maintaining your stranglehold on this seeming identity,
What can anyone do?

You say that you are here seeking freedom.
Without the freedom to disentangle yourself from
The conditionings of past generations,
What freedom can be had?

Your world is the expression of your beingness.
If you are not, your world is not.

Establish your priorities.
You cannot transcend the world while at the same time
Being in relentless pursuit of it.
Every attachment is another set of restraints.
How many attachments can you hold on to
While expecting freedom?

The world is not essential to your happiness.
What is essential to your happiness is the Essential.
The only true rest is inside.
Fixated on what is outside,
One never gains true rest.

The body has a degree of importance only because
The Energy operates through it.

Nothing at all that is from you is you.
Identity is all that constitutes 'me'.
The extension of identity into the world is named 'mine'.

This form has been granted a finite amount of energy.

The more energy that goes into the reinforcement of identity,
The less that is available for clarity.
You are not born with a self;
It is something you acquire and build on.

Master, why is all this so difficult?

A sculptor's job is much easier than Wu Hsin's.
To him, the stone offers no resistance.
Most of the visitors who climb the mountain to come here
Merely desire to amass more knowledge.
They are like children that don't understanding
The dangers in gorging themselves on sweet rice.

Recognition

Today begins with a cautionary word, Xu Fengqin.

Wu Hsin can talk about the true state of affairs.
But each must see it for himself.
Drink the words.
Keep analyzing until ultimately thinking itself ceases and
You go beyond all thought.

Rather than continuing to perpetuate what isn't,
You now open to What-Is.
You re-cognize what you were before even
Your parents were born.

It is seeing a wholeness of oneSelf,
Reality in its totality and myriad diversity.
This holistic dynamic of being and knowing,
That which no statement or answered question can reach,
Can be apperceived from an unmediated source.

Standing outside of the narrative entitled 'Me in this world',
What is discerned is the unified functioning of the Totality as
A singular inviolate continuum containing everything:
Both the impermanent and the permanent,
Duality and non-duality, illusion and reality,
Self and other than self.

What one is is like space.
What one appears to be is like
The space in a hut.
When the hut is disassembled,
The space is unaffected.

As such, this body is not 'me'.
It is mine as I am that which uses it.
This mind is not 'me'.
It is mine as I am that which knows it.

What am I?
I am not even I.
I am that 'no thing' which I points to.

The cessation of identification with
That which had presumed to be 'me' allows
The authentic-I to shine forth.
This clear point of view is
Not one of seeking, sequentially through experiences,
But of piercing the veiling and
Penetrating directly into What-Is.

In that instant, the entire principle which has served as
The center of your so-called life will have disappeared.

Life continues on,
A life of participation without involvement,
Where the game is what's important and not its outcome.

The body is cared for in the same manner that
One who nurses cares for a patient.
Without any sense of possessiveness.
Yet, her duties are performed quite normally.

This realization of the higher cannot be accomplished without
One's release of one's grasping of the lower.
Just as the body is changing,
The seeming self is changing and
Its world is likewise changing.

The entire frame of reference is based on

The triad of the body,
What is inside it and
What is outside it.
Take away the body and
What is the significance of inside and outside?

The Self-search is the search for
That which is always already present.
How difficult can finding It be as long as
You are willing to sift
The essential from the non-essential?

One must discriminate between That which is and
That which appears to be.
What relationship can there be between them?

The body moves from place to place,
But is never away from
That which is everywhere.

A few are unerringly aware of this while most are not.

Take shelter under that which has been
Providing such shelter to you for your entire life.
Acknowledge That and become devoted to That.

All you need is already within you.
Passively allow attention to settle spontaneously into
The sense of Being,
That which sources attention, self,
Body-mind, and all phenomena.

Don't concern yourself with enlightenment.
Enlightenment happens when there is
A need for it to happen.
Therefore, no one makes it happen.

The Totality alone satisfies the need.
In silence and stillness,
Inquire into the ultimate meaning of the common referent 'I'.
Do not succumb to impatience.
See the world as a series of streaming objects only and
YourSelf as the sole Subject.

This is the transformation of
The unconscious union with the Source to
A conscious one.
The only thing that stands in the way are one's thoughts.

Wu Hsin recommends the disengaging of attention
From the senses by turning attention within, and then
Emptying consciousness of all content.

This 'going within' is actually a 'going out' of oneself.
The experience of selfhood,
Being a construction of mind is
Naturally eroded when the mind's activity is slowed.

The greater the resultant void,
The greater the radiance of the Self.

When the mind is silent,
Everything disappears and
What remains is nothing.
This nothing can also be given up,
But the one who gives it up remains.

What is the difference between Consciousness and my consciousness?

'My' consciousness is particularized consciousness whereas
Consciousness is undifferentiated.

Now let us stop here, Xu Fengqin.

Consider these things until next we meet.

This day, the Master said:
The choice is an easy one.

You are obsessed with and immersed in phenomena or
You are immersed in yourSelf.
The individual is always creating relationship,
Me and other.
There can be no relationship with yourSelf.

It's never about somebody finding something other than
The finding of somebody's absence.

Act as if you have a choice.
You have a body in the same way as
You have a cart.
They are yours,
Yet not you.

You are the sun,
Not an object that the sun gives light to.
Death is not non-being;
Death is non-being something in particular.

When your body ends,
All that was perceived and experienced
Through the body likewise ends.
What continues is what was
Before the arrival of the body,
The real you.

But Master, the world continues.

What evidence do you have of that?

Many people have died but the world obviously continues.

These people all died in your world.
You and your world are a unit.
They come and go together.
You see yourself in the world, while
Wu Hsin sees the world in himself.

The traditional schools advocate the study of scripture.
But believing that awakening
Can be brought about through scripture is
Like hoping to find fresh water in dried fish.

The main difficulty is in experientially realizing
What has been intellectually understood.
The paradox of awakening is that it is both gradual and sudden.

It is like termites gnawing away at a tree.
Eating, gnawing, eating;
Suddenly the tree falls.

Thoughts in Mind

Master Wu Hsin began his instruction:
Realize that every experience,
What is seen or heard, touched or smelled,
Felt or thought, expected or imagined, is
Generated in the mind and isn't the actual.

Only your sense 'I am',
Though in the world, is not of the world.
Once you can take your position outside of the world,
The desire to change it will fall away.

When you were three,
You didn't look like you do today.
The three-year-old's behaviors are not
The same as yours nor are its thoughts.
Granted, its name is the same
But surely that can't be all of it.
So what is it that makes it you, Xu Fengqin?

You can visit a river every day and take it to be the same.
However, upon reflection,
It is obvious that it is not.
The water that comprised the river yesterday is not
The river's water today.

In the same way,
What you are today is not
What you were yesterday, appearances notwithstanding.

Should you just accept that
This identity is a constant movement and

Leave it at that?
Or do you continue to dive deeper,
To fathoms that you have yet to fathom?

That you exist and that
You know that you exist cannot be challenged.
We are here only to look at
What else can be known you are with certainty.

Mind is the site of a singular current of mental activity,
A reflecting surface as it were,
Onto which thoughts appear and dissolve.

What is the role of the Mind?

The organism separates the private "inside" self from
That other vast expanse "outside."
Selfhood serves as the interface with "other",
With the world outside.

No sense of unity or wholeness must get passed the mind that
Would challenge or threaten the separateness which is
The underlying supposition of the self-reference.

Personal existence is a process.
Personal existence is not that of an entity.
The seeming I is an activity,
Not an object, and not a fixed and eternally defined subject.
The process is temporary and is dependent a human form.

This individual arises, changes, and passes.
It is the same process that is duplicated as
Infinite possible variations of human persons.
The process that is "I" is
Integrated as a "person" while it persists, and then
It is disintegrated into the Universal.

The mind is constantly reconstructing representations that
Stand in reference to the external world.
Often there is a whole set of deceptions that are going on;
There is filling in missing information, or
Creating experiences which are not exactly matched to reality.
In that sense, an external world is nothing other than simulation.

Perception is a story.
One integrates information into meaningful models of the world,
To include previous experiences which are
Brought to bear upon perception.

The activity of thought is to
Interpret that which the senses take in by
Dividing the impressions into relative elements.
This is done for physical survival.

All that is personal appears and disappears.
What is perceived is a self-generated world, a mirage.
Once you have seen the mirage to be mirage,
Only one with weak conviction will continue to go to it to
Quench their thirst.

All phenomena are registered.
None are categorized, labeled or compared.
With self-consciousness,
Everything that is taken in is weighed against
How does this relate to "me"?

This is seeing from a fabricated center.

Am I my mind?

The mind is an appearance;
It appears to you.

It comes and goes.
That which is the essential continuous is
Something other than the mind.

Is the mind different from consciousness?

The mind appears in consciousness
Like a cloud appears in the sky.
There is consciousness of the mind.
Mindfulness of consciousness points to consciousness.

Objects appear in consciousness.
Once the recognition of consciousness is clearly stabilized,
Look at that too.

Identification with objects is
The surest sign of confusion, of
Not knowing who you are.
What you are is prior to
The appearance of thoughts, of objects, of all phenomena.

Resting there, confusion dissolves.

Shall I consider it to be my enemy?

No, the mind is not the enemy,
It is a tool.
Use it when you need to, like a shovel.
But don't treat every condition as if it were a hard earth.

What you are is antecedent to the mind.
This makes recognizing your true nature through the mind impossible.
Setting the mind aside clears the way for a
Direct confrontation with appearances and
The ensuing Self-recognition.

What are you?
You are the reflection of what you think about.

In that sense,
You are responsible for the conflicts in your life.
When the movement toward becoming 'something other' ceases,
You end the self-created conflict with yourself.

Then and only then,
You can make an inner shift of interest and attention
Away from the unessential and
Establish your refuge in the Energy,
Trusting in Its goodwill toward you.

You don't know what is good;
You know only what is good for you.
Everything is framed in relation to
This "you" that has been created.

Self-centric thought is merely a protective mechanism,
A program to protect and promote the self-interests at all costs.

The basic conflict is that you demand an identity whereas
Your essential nature is without one.
There is movement away from the essence and
Toward what seems more comfortable, identity.

The sense I-am calls out for definition:
What am I?

That is the start of the identification process,
The creation of an individuated form of consciousness and
The attachment of things to it.

Over time, the identities change,

But the demand for identification does not.
You assume that you are continuous, Xu Fengqin,
But how do you know?

Might you truly be intermittent?
And if you are not, what is?

You are afraid of ending, yet
The only thing that ends is
The construction that fears the ending.

Self-centric thought seems to be continuous,
It too is intermittent.
It has created a parallel realm into which
You retreat away from reality every day.
Every day, it seems as if the
Arrival of the sun wipes out the stars.
But that's only how it seems.

Begin by clarifying the distinction between mind and Mind.

A sequential stream of thoughts is mind.
The screen they appear on is Mind,
Which is illuminated by Consciousness.

The mind can be further divided into
Functioning mind and self-fixated mind wherein
The former services the operation of the organism and
The latter services the seeming self.

What you appear to be,
What you are conditioned to think you are
But are not, is temporal.
What you call your self is
Some thought, emotion or sensation that
You are temporarily identified with.

When you awaken in the morning,
What wakes up first?

'I am' wakes up.
Then, the sensing systems wake up.
From there, "I-am-this", me, and
"There is that", the world, arise.

You are constantly trying to be this or that,
To achieve a particular state,
To capture one kind of experience and avoid another.

Sometimes you accept the unnecessary and
Reject the necessary.
All too frequently, what you want
Causes you to reject what you need.

What is needed is the discernment that
Thinking and becoming are both limited and
Can therefore never take you to the unlimited.

Simply be aware: "I am not the body,
I am not the mind.
I am simply pure awareness."

As this awareness deepens,
The mind's impact on you loses all force.
When the awareness is fully settled,
The self-centric mind simply evaporates.
This is not an outcome or a proficiency
Brought about through practice.
It is the spontaneous apperception of
What always already is,
The Most Antecedent.

My efforts to move beyond mind have all met with failure. What is lacking?

If the body cannot free you from your mind and
The mind can't free you from the mind,
What is left to work with?

The problem lies in wrong assumption,
Suggesting that one needs to be freed from mind.

The eyes observe the world.
The mind observes the eyes.
Consciousness observes the mind.
The Absolute Observes Consciousness.

Free attention is the spotlight of Consciousness.
When it is entangled in the contents of the mind,
It is no longer free, Xu Fengqin.

When the contents of the mind are no longer 'mine',
Then the right relationship with mind has been established.
Mind can then be observed,
But there is no identification with it.

Identification results in a seeming personalized consciousness.
The self-centricity is
A viewing of the world from the perspective of a body.

Then, the expanded self uses possessions to
Announce to others its own sense of identity.
This construction of identity usually begins with
The use of 'I', 'me', and 'mine'.

Before self-consciousness,
There is consciousness witnessing.

Self-consciousness dawns and identifies itself via
The first thought appearing: I.
Then, every thing witnessed is referenced against the identity;
'I-me-mine' becomes second nature.

The self-reference exists;
It only doesn't exist as it's been described,
As an entity.

If the endless voice which
You listen to inside your head is
The product of something that is nonexistent,
What does that say about your mental state?

The issue at hand is
The arbitrary and uninspected identification of
A seeming personal consciousness,
A sense of entity, with the varieties of experience.
The drive for a self-fulfillment via experience
Reflects the self-actuating reward mechanisms in operation.

The self-reference will never leave you.
You have to leave it by seeing yourself as distinct from it,
By seeing yourself as the witness of both
The content-free state and the state with content.

You are that antecedent Being Conscious Presence.
What is required is an in-turning,
An inner shift of interest away from the personal and
Toward the source of the personal
Resulting in the reassertion of
The primacy of universal consciousness.

Whatever arises does so spontaneously.
The mirror can only show what is already there.

The in-turning involves the
Recognizing and allowing of whatever arises
Rather than their resistance and exclusion.
There is no longer any opposition to "other".

The result is a spontaneous recognition.
Since it is acausal,
There is nothing to practice.
The only thing to do is recognize what you essentially are.
From I-am-this, one goes to I-am so that
One may ultimately free oneself from it
As luminous I.

Within this, it is important to draw a distinction
Between the suppression of thought and
The suspension of thought.
The former is a type of violence, of one aspect of life
Seeking control over another.

If the attention is firmly fixed on Being,
Whether or not the flow of thoughts continues becomes unimportant.

The ability to concentrate on a single thought is
Inferior to the inability to hold on to any thought.
Always seeking to develop abilities,
One overlooks the value of this inability.

Wu Hsin is not addressing
The use of the mind in any pursuit,
Regardless of how lofty it may be.
What he refers to is the freeing of attention,
The detaching of attention from
The phenomena it had fixed upon.

It is a cessation of grasping,

Even of grasping awakening.
Free attention simply observes without commentary or evaluation.

This freed attention takes in everything.
Usually, attention is mostly selective
Based on presumed value assigned by the intellect.

See for yourself, Xu Fengqin.
How much more interest is there in what is 'mine'
Than there is in any thing 'not mine'?

Master, it has been my experience that the cessation of thought is very difficult.

There is a changeless 'I' underlying every 'mine'.
The mind you call 'yours' provides
The screen on which the entire world appears.

The mind-flow is quite strong as
A raging river is strong.
Either can carry you away.

The knower of the mind merely observes;
It does not interfere in anything.
Soon, you will see that the nearer you get to Reality,
The more you lose interest in your worldly affairs.

Not becoming anything is the key.
Becoming is merely the movement from
Being one thing to being another thing.

I believe this is enough for today, my son.
The Master concluded.

After the morning meal, the Master began:

The purpose today will be to
Clarify the basic posture or point of view.
Here, we integrate the positive way with the negative way.

Wu Hsin addresses both what you are and what you aren't.
Knowing what you are and what you aren't are
Two roads leading to the same address.

At times, an intellectual understanding develops.
Wu Hsin is not suggesting that there is a causal relationship
Between intellectual understanding and Recognition.
However, there is a high correlation between
An intellectual understanding and deeper insight.

Start with the re-directing of attention.
You are.
This fact of being is key.
Before anything can appear,
You're already there.
Before any narrative can be constructed,
You are already present.

Thoughts, perceptions, sensations and images come and go.
They are experienced.
Don't confuse yourself, Xu Fengqin, to be any of these.
You are the Observing of them.

They're are all appearances to you.
Look to see what this that you already are is.

The authentic-I is that subjective reality which
Underlies the individual "I" and
Allows for the experience of "I-amness" as one's existence.
It is the authentic-I that enables the statement, "I."

Seek to know It,
Not to know about It.

This moves you out of the intellectual and
Into pure Knowing.
Is your own existence an inference or
Is it self-evident?
It is doesn't need to be proved,
Because it's clear, it's obvious,
It's always already.

Thought cannot know.
Thought can only think it knows.
This is the basis for confusion.

Now, before you present any question, stop.
Formulate it from the perspective that
This will be the question that ends all questions.
Questions that lead to other questions are endless,
Leaving the questioner still adrift.

Then why am I not aware of the authentic-I all the time?

You are, but it is overlooked in your fixation on the world.
Whatever comes and goes is mere appearance to you.
You are prior to any appearance as
The substrate on which it appears.
Confusion is introduced by attempting to
Grasp what you are through structure.
The world appears in you,
On the screen of consciousness.

Your real nature is prior to and
Beyond all notions and formulations.
What you are is beyond all concepts, and hence
Beyond all categories.

There exists an insufficient clarity surrounding
The things you know you know,
The things you do not know, and
The ones you don't know you don't know.

Man has established a false certainty to
Support himself in the uncertain world.
As such, belief is a content-independent process
Which results in confusion.

For belief,
No evidence is required.
You take the world to be outside you
Whereas it is actually in you.
You don't go to it;
It comes to you.

You base your identity on objects when in fact
You are the only subject.
You have accepted what seems to be for what actually is.
You have accepted your answers without questioning them and
This is what needs to be undone.

Master, I have listened most attentively, yet the illusion continues to seem so real?

As the world of the dream appears in the mind, so too,
The world of the waking state is
An appearance in mind only.
Mind is where images appear.
You are always back where you started because
You never go outside of it.

All spatiotemporal phenomena are delusive superimpositions.
The Primary Delusion is that these superimpositions
Objectify not only the spatiotemporal world but,

Yourself as a thing amongst things in that world.

What is difficult for you to embrace is that
What you are is nothing perceivable.
You are nothing that you are conscious of.

The only way to know this ephemerality is by its effects.
Energy moving through water is called wave.
Energy moving through the air is called wind.
Don't lose this important perspective.

Man takes what he believes to be fact and
Takes what he perceives to be real.
There is no alternative for you but to
Accept the world as a mere imagination.
Unless you give up the idea that
The world is anything other than an appearance,
You will always pursue it.

Taking the appearance to be real,
You will never know the Real Itself.

To fully experience the ocean,
You have to take your clothes off.
To dive deeply into oneSelf,
The clothes or uniform that
Constitute the seeming self must go.

Drop your present identity and
Embrace the paradox of identification with this formlessness.

What must become evident is that
The Energy is everything.
Subjectively, It is Knowing and Acting or Moving.
Objectively, it is the world and the body therein.

There is neither a "me" nor its narrative
To be found anywhere other than in imagination.
Yet, there is a sense of being that is
The same in everyone;
It is universal.

When the drinking glass breaks,
The in-formed portion of the space is
Reabsorbed into the universal space.
Similarly, when any living form breaks down,
The Energy that was in it is
Simply reabsorbed into Itself.

Before one can go beyond consciousness,
One must arrive at consciousness.
The perspective from the mountaintop is
Different from that of the valley.

People believe that consciousness
Requires a mind and body.
What you are in reality is
Prior to being anything in particular.

You are Knowing,
The shapeless Subject,
The irreducible substrate of the visible and the invisible, of
The subjective and the objective, and of
Form and the formless.

This Subjectivity is the ever-present,
Both in the presence and absence of any phenomena.

Confusion

Confusion is a unique disease;
No other is as incurable as
The idea of being an individual.

Confusion is where unchanging Being is
Perceived and experienced as impermanent becoming.
Confusion is the conflict between a fact and
What is taken as a fact.

An action that is rooted in confusion must, by necessity,
Perpetuate the confusion.
It should be obvious, Xu Fengqin, that
In the absence of a point of view,
A referential center,
Facts can be seen clearly.

In such an absence,
There can be no confusion between
What you are and what you appear to be.

Being has no agenda,
No intended outcome.
It is passive whereas
Becoming is about actions to provide outcomes.

Any form of self-improvement is really
The perpetuation of "me" in different forms.
Essentially it is the continuance of the "me" as
A new and improved, a refined, "me".

What causes confusion?

Confusion is the wrongful ideation that either
Exaggerates or underestimates the actual nature of things.

Viewing the world in fragments is like trying to understand
The individual pieces of a puzzle.
A wrong view of the world must consequently arise,
One that has distorted and skewed What-Is.

The primary confusion is misidentification.
Misidentification is the condition where
There is the confusing of Self with not-Self.
Its reversal is awakening,
The dissolution of the entanglement between
Experiencing and Its instrument.

Maintain the attention on being,
On consciousness, on presence,
On the Knowing of the content.

One must provide water to a plant until
It develops roots.
Then it grows by itself.
Likewise, study these words until they take root.
Then understanding grows at its own pace.

Understand that the 'within' is only relative to the 'without'.
Without a 'without',
There can be no 'within'.

All there is:
One with One,
One from One,
One in One.

No distinction, no multiplicity either, only One.

Even in total darkness, It is shining.
To try to describe It is even more difficult that
Trying to describe music.

Wu Hsin's instruction is now drawing to a close.
After five moons have passed,
We will come together one last time and
It will be concluded.

Therefore, deeply consider all that has been said and
If anything remains unclear,
It shall be clarified.

Final Day

That about which nothing can be said,
Wu Hsin has now said.

Written or spoken words can only describe
That which must be directly experienced.
The berry can never be sweet until it is tasted.

Time spent with Wu Hsin is only for
Hearing the words and
Establishing a mind-to-mind resonance.

Wu Hsin has given you this wisdom, Xu Fengqin.
It is beyond the mind and intellect.
Because Wu Hsin's words are true,
What he advises comes true.

When the attention is no longer attached to objects,
That which has been previously veiled by the objects is unveiled.
To discern What-Is,
One must extinguish the fire of what-is-not.

There is no need to grudgingly continue to suppress
The fullness of conscious existence.
You are not stuck with a mind that
Seems to be inside and separate from the world.

Wu Hsin acknowledges that
You are in constant struggle with
The paradox of your wanting reality and
Being scared of it at the same time.

To date, you have been unable to reconcile
That which you are with that which you seem to be.
What you are is not perceivable;
What you seem to be is a name with a distinct form, and
An accompanying narrative.

They would appear to be irreconcilable yet
It is their very reconciliation that constitutes awakening.
Begin with the understanding that
The Energy is acting through a particular form.
There is total functioning through
Billions and billions of such distinct forms.

The Energy has brought you here,
To make you seek out Wu Hsin.

You already have
The intuition of a Transcendental Consciousness.
Were this not the case,
You'd be whoring right now.

You have only one problem.
It is the involvement with body and mind and the narrative.
In the absence of any involvement,
Where is the problem?

Concede that this person that
You claim you are is objectively observable.
Discriminate between that which observes and the observed.
Can you see that whatever you observe
Points to your existence as a center of observation?

Can you see that whatever you experience
Points to your existence as a center of experiencing?

The awareness of the world is conditional,

It requires perception or cognition and an instrument for them.
It becomes obvious that only when you are that
The world comes into existence.

'I am this body with this mind' is an idea.
Replace it with another idea.
The development of the conviction "I am the Energy" will serve you well.
Hold the thought "I am the Energy" until such time as
There is no need to remind yourself.

Now, what say you, Xu Fengqin?
Are there matters unresolved?
Are there any questions remaining?

No, Master Wu Hsin.
The greatness of your instruction has taken me to
The brink of my mind and then beyond.

As a result of our time together,
I am profoundly and directly aware of what I am.
It is a direct knowledge in consciousness itself,
Consciousness without the additions to consciousness.

I am the nature and support of all things.

It is obvious that
The entire universe is mind-made,
Existing only in consciousness,
Whereas I am that which is observing consciousness.

I have met my Self and through this meeting,
It is now clear that all this,
I am.
I am everywhere.
I am one, while

Appearing as one amongst many.

I am the seen, the seer and
The light by which all is seen.

I am that by which all things are known,
That by which all things are possible,
That in which both transcendent and immanent resolve,
That by which Being is sourced,
That to which there is neither entry nor exit, and
That which gods worship.

This body is a temporal sensation.
It is only a covering on Me.
It enables Me to know the world and move and act in it.
What do any event have to do with Me?

I know this and
This conviction is unshakable.
I am like a man drinking freshly brewed tea
Who knows in himself how hot it is.

There are no words to express the profound gratitude I am feeling.
As such, I must remain silent.

How is it that you know that your understanding is final?

The understanding is final because
The understanding is not property and
Cannot be viewed to be mine.
It is That Which Is.

There are no subject/object distinctions, nor
Any other distinctions among
Parts of the singular whole.
The entity I thought I was has dissolved.

Master, there is no more to realize.
In truth, it is impossible to communicate.
It eludes all words and familiar descriptive categories.
As such, I must remain silent.

What will you do now, Xu Fengqin?

Master, I cannot say.
The body will go where it is moved to go and will
Act as it is moved to act.
'I' is gone.
'Me' is gone.
'Mine' is gone.
Having no input in the matter,
It is best if I remain silent.

OTHER WU HSIN TRANSLATIONS BY ROY MELVYN

An Interlude in Eternity

Aphorisms for Thirsty Fish

Behind the Mind

Being Conscious Presence

In the Shadow of the Formless

Mindless Understanding

No Great Future Attainment

No Other to Each Other

Recognition of the Obvious

Solving Yourself: Yuben de Wu Hsin

The Magnificence of the Ordinary

Made in the USA
San Bernardino, CA
28 November 2015